# The Reality of the Heart

by

Chandriss Gates

Copyright ©2020 Chandriss Gates

All rights reserved. No part of this publication may be reproduced, distributed, or transmitted in any form or by any means, including photocopying, recording, or other electronic or mechanical methods, without the prior written permission of the publisher, except in the case of brief quotations embodied in critical reviews and certain other noncommercial uses permitted by copyright law.

ISBN-978-1-951300-18-0

Liberation's Publishing – West Point - Mississippi

# Dedication

*This book is dedicated to my true self*

# Table of Content

Fearing of Love ............................................................. 7

Feelings Within ............................................................. 8

Mommy Bear ............................................................. 10

Something Real ........................................................... 11

Secret Dreams ............................................................. 12

Fire and Cold ............................................................... 14

Silent Cry ..................................................................... 16

Sad Song ..................................................................... 18

Dumb because of You ................................................. 20

What's within your heart ............................................. 17

Love of Fear ................................................................ 24

Shatter Picture ............................................................. 22

My own Destiny .......................................................... 25

Cage Bird ..................................................................... 26

Love Game .................................................................. 27

Are You My Reality ............................................. 28

Honey ................................................................. 30

A Fools Heart ..................................................... 32

Faded Smile ....................................................... 29

Silent Heart ........................................................ 33

Snowflake Love ................................................. 35

Lost Call ............................................................. 36

Can you feel? ..................................................... 37

Fiction or Fact ................................................... 38

Broken Angel ..................................................... 39

Shadow Knight .................................................. 40

My Lonely Star .................................................. 41

Love me like you Love you ............................... 42

Feels of Unwanted Love ................................... 44

## Fearing of Love

They love me, without the same
hears as me.

Aren't the words of a man
truer than a woman's?

If so, why did those words
feel so empty as they came
from your mouth.

Putting a hole where my
heart should be.

I silently think why I love you
without a true heart?

Within my cold heart, there's a
voice, looking for help.

Silently I looked for that love when
it wasn't given to me

I shut you out without thinking
Twice.

My heart closed without saying
a word to you.

## Feelings Within

I'll normally side along against
the world.

Knowing my fears will come
to haunt me like a wild animal.

No matter how hard I try to lock
Away the key, as if it was ever that
easy to do,

You just stood there looking puzzled
as if I was speaking with no language
as if my actions had no meaning.

You said a long time ago,

You would help me with the nightmares
that came to my mind.

It seems to me you are the nightmares
I have feared within.

Can't you see I'm not breathing
When I'm near you?

But you are still here killing me
with your words of emptiness.

No words you speak will come close to the
Truth that you might try to tell me.

I shut you out as if a steel door
Appeared.

You look at me with tears in your eyes.

I smile softly as I close the door.

Before I close them, I look up at you
Once again to see your face so I can
remember it.

"I'm sorry for blocking you. It's just I
Can't be my true self when you're around"

So, I say to you once more, goodbye inner fear.

Sincerely – Inner Fear

# Mommy Bear

My life wouldn't be right without you.

You have been with me when no one would dare to look at me.

So, I thank you, Mama.

Your love was all I needed in my time of need.

Your words smoothed over any rough thoughts that came to my mind.

My mouth knew when to speak and when not to speak.

So, I thank you for everything.

I love you, Mama

## *Something* **Real**

I shut myself away from you for
a reason.

Why do you still fight to protect me?

The monster you see before you isn't
a creature to be kept hidden.

My inner fear controls my life
when it comes down to you.

Show me something that no one
dares to show me.

Would you show me the world
that I want the most?

Make me feel like somebody.

## *Secret* **Dreams**

Do I dare to close my eyes to
dream a better dream?

Nothing came along until I
thought of you.

My mind filled with wonderful
things about you.

As I lay down cuddling up
within my covers

I wonder some more.

Why can't I tell you about
the feelings that I don't tell
or show anyone?

You have something that
I want.

I won't lose it over something
Stupid.

But only if you want me to
Lose it, I will.

But my dreams are simple. You've

just got to put the pieces
together.

Goodnight, Sweet Dreams

I love you

## Fire and Cold

Your heart is what's keeping
me here with you.

Only you, everywhere I look,
I see the coldness in their eyes.

But as I look into yours
I see love.

Hold me tight as we fight
against the world.

Just me and you.

Us leaving those people
where they stand.

It's not like the world
Isn't enough for us?

But your smile warms up my
day even when you're cold as ice.

I'll love you until the end
Of the world.

## *falling* for You

As my heart speaks
The word
"I love you"

You may know
It's true, but
Your heart

Tell you don't
Love another
Soul

But you look
Me in my eyes
And they speak
Words that never
Come to mind

Let the love come
To play as you
Can breathe
Something real

## Silent Cry

The ground below my feet

isn't capable for me to walk on.

I'll stand here waiting for it to

carry me while I stand still

as the Color of the sky.

My eyes are closed as the darkness

take controls my mind.

I'm not going to be able to show

the love I once thought I had to.

I'll cry silently to myself, but no one

around me will see the tears coming

down my face.

I'll scream and scream

But this time no one will come to

my rescue.

## What's Within Your Heart

Reality is hard to grasp
within this world of ours

Why can't we say what we really feel about
our significant other now days?

Why can't can we?

I wonder why we can't say what's
on our heart.

How do you really feel about me?

How do you REALLY feel about me?

I can't see why my heart aches for you.
You can't say what's upon your heart.

Why can't you just say what you feel.
The words you speak and the words you don't speak
are still words all the same.

## Sad Song

You and I can't

be apart for

anything in the

World.

Let's start tonight

Just me and you

Against the cold

world .

Without

You I'm just a

Sad song.

Looking back at

The memories we

Shared together.

Now, you are gone

from my grasp.

And now I

Can't hold your

Hand to hold on.

Without you

I'm just a sad song

## *Dumb* Because of You

I'm just a woman
Of my word.

I really do feel dumb

for falling for you.

Anything you do

I'll go right

along with it.

Without a second

Thought of worries

Even when everyone

Said throw you to

The curve,

When things change
I'll stay with you
Even though you're

Broke…broke
…broke…

I'm still dumb for

Loving you.

I'm dumb when I'm
Talking to you.

But it's because
I love you.

You're the only
On I want.

…say you dumb
Because of me…

# Shattered Picture

What's the best way to escape from the pain we feel
within our heart?
Why do we try to touch someone who is so
untouchable?
We end up getting our hearts broken
with tears rolling down our face.

Why do I cry for you when you never shed a tear
Except when you were saying sorry for hurting me?

Why do I want only your love and nobody else's?
No love can be compared to yours.
Only your love will make me feel whole again.

Am I a fool for loving, or
was I a fool for giving my heart to you?
A heart that has never been fully touched by another
soul.

A fool I am…
I believe so baby,
Why can't you see you're hurting me with the words
you said to me?

"we're better off as friends"
"let's take a break"

These words alone are toxic to my heart

You hold in your hands what lets me heal.

I stand before you a shattered picture of what's broken or hurting within me.

## Love of Fear

My reality is shattering once again right before my eyes.
Why does this world haunt me with what it calls love?

Love is just a dream we try to catch within this twisted reality we call home or even the world.

Why can't I just feel your love without the negative thoughts of you leaving my side?
I don't want you as a friend but as my lover, which you are.

My heart aches only for you in this twisted world we live in.
You, just you, are the only thing on mind.

While I'm just trying to pick the pieces up where the hole still is within my heart.
Only your smile fills my heart up with something new.

# My own Destiny

Let the flow of the wind take
All our pain away baby.
Let's take our mind off of all the worries
of this world.

Hold my hand and let's walk down the path
together.
Not as individual people but as one baby.

We know the pain of being in love.
I'm here now…
I've always been here beside you visible or not.

It's alright to hold back but know
I'm always here for you through the
pain and the love.

Let's fight against what's holding
us back from having what we want.
In this reality baby

So, can we go now baby.

## Caged Bird

Let the pain of your past be free from your heart

Show this world the true beauty of you

smile and glow

Never be down with the sadness of the past within your heart

Be free and show
The little love that's within your heart

# Love Game

The game of love is like…
A game of dice

Why should we play along and
take chances for nothing in return?

Let's play together
Eye for eye or to the death.

The world will not give you a free chance
to play its true game.
So, let's take a chance for something small.

Reality is just a dream for the naked eye.
It's just a deception created by the mind.
The only belief we have is what we see with the eye.

We dream of love,
but in the pursuit of it
It left us with an empty hole
Where we once dreamed of only love

In your mind,
Your heart,
And maybe even your soul

## Are You My Reality

Why do I feel heart ache when
you say I love you, are you my toxic lover
Or my lonely soul mate?

Why do I only want your love and attention?
Why do I only want your touch?

Just your touch alone
Can cause so much pain
While I cry longing for you
And only you.

Can you be the one I've been craving?

The love I never had from any man
I have ever met before.

# faded Smile

Let the world know
How you felt so many
Years ago.

Why keep your tears
held inside not healing
Anything?

Give me a reason to say
"I love you"

My heart gives my words
Meaning
They come from
The heart.

Break my heart once
Or maybe twice

The meaning will fade away
With my smile

## Honey

The trembling vibration of your body
Makes me powerful, but just like me
You're scared.

I lay you down on the bed
And kiss down your neck

With gentle touches of your hand on my head,
Leading my head downward to take care of your needs

Every sound with you feels ecstatic and satisfying
As if I'm laying with a god

This feeling is something new that I never felt.
Maybe it's love,
If so, I shall keep quiet until the time is right

Maybe this is only love that you need for a moment

Let the moment fill the air
As you please me baby
Touch my skin softly as you kiss takes control

As you rub my body you take
Gentle care of my needs
You kiss down my stomach
To my wonderland

Rubbing her with kindness

You climb on top ready to take control
You say to me "why stop here when the fun hasn't even started yet"
My body felt warmth that it hasn't felt before

Let my body feel the love
In more ways than one
Show me the true meaning of love

# A Fool's Heart

Hey baby, why have you changed?
Is it that you want something new?
Or is it that your true colors are
Showing right before my eyes.

Why do I only want you?
No one else can make me smile
Just by saying so little to me.

Am I a fool for your love
or a fool who will do anything
to feel loved?

Was my love no good to you?
Or is my love not good enough for you?

Can you tell me the truth
how you really feel for me

Or…

Will I forever be a fool for you?

## Silent Heart

Can you love me when I
Don't love myself?
Are you
Really the one for me?

When you tell me you love me,
the look in your eyes says
You are saying it to someone else.

I thought I was the one for you?
The words you are telling me now
are more hurtful than the ones before.

Just love me with all my flaws.
I know dealing with me is hard,
But the work always pays off

Do you really love me
the way I love you?

Don't hold back the love
you want to give me?
I'll return it with love you
never had before.

So just love me and
I'll love you back

I'll forever be your lover

Sincerely-The Heart

# *Snowflake* Love

Why do you want my love
When you act as if you do not care if you're
with or without me?

Be real with me and yourself.
What do you desire from me?
Is it my love, my time, my affection?

What is love?
Love today is controlled by madness and lies,
The love I have for you baby is pure
and it's real.

Can you really say you love me when your
eyes are cold as ice?

I just want the truth.
But the madness around us says
there are lies being covered up.
What I guess I want to hear and even…
feel is…

Can you love me the way your words sound?
Can you change my mindset from the past, baby?
I just want you and only you
But you are pushing me
Away with the past.

## Lost Call

I forgot once upon
A time I use to be
Lost...Myself...

But being in the dark
Doesn't mean my cries
Weren't heard by you
Or anyone.

Show me...my mistakes.

I lost my call once before
But now I see you and my call
Has been found again.

Let's never get lost
...Again...

Just only in our dreams and
Where our dreams come to
Life.

Never again will my call be
Heard from another phone
Or soul

Just yours and only yours...

## Can You Feel?

Let my love reach out to you.
Can you not see the love I have
for you,
Can you let me love you?

I'm standing here ten toes
down for you and only you.

I step out so much for you
But my efforts are useless.

Can you love me the way you
Feel me or the way you see reality
In those lonely eyes?

I want to love you endlessly
But the feelings I have are
starting to fade away more and
More.
A painful tear runs down
My face.

Can't you stop the pain I feel
or am I forever stuck looking
behind you while holding my
head dead down crying in silence

## *fiction* or Fact

Reality is just an illusion
Of our mind.
We just
go along with it because
we don't know what's real.

Can we say that
illusion is
Just a reality or
just the reality
we were forced upon?

Let my heart weigh down upon
my hands until your hands

You are my protector.

Can you do the job that
You are facing now?

# Broken Angel

The toughness of your skin, the beating
Sound of your heart, the warmth of
Your love is all any man should ever want.

But from all the heartache the world
had brought,
It's amazing that your heart isn't torn apart.

But for the pain you keep bolted down
Inside like a safe, only grows and causes
More pain… for the fear of heartache
Is only one step away

You try your best to hide the pain
And try to cry silently at night awake

For this brings me more pain… for the
Tears of my angel is more than I can take

Don't let the devil take control of your heart
Because he just wants to destroy what you have
Built and survive to be in this reality we call Earth…

Let it be known that our love is strong so let
The tears of joy fall…

From your heavenly face my angel let
The true love comes out to play

# Shadow Knight

Why are you so close, but yet so far away?
It's your shadow that keeps the light away

Your shadow keeps me wide awake seeing
it makes my body shake in fear.

The terror that make a child shed tears
Seeing it keeps me in a state of paralysis.
Or the feeling of begin pinned down by a
Million past decisions.

Is it my fault that you stuck around?
Is it the fear I have of you the thing
That's keeping me bound?

Or maybe it is you that sticks around
Because your fears of me never wanting
To be around is the thing that makes you
Frown

The shadow figure I see in the middle
Of the knight is now afraid of me...

So am I know the figure in the knight,
Or the figure of light

# 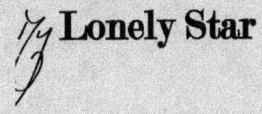Lonely Star

Even during the night, I see you
As bright as a star.
Do you feel me
Staring without you here with me

Can you feel my love here upon earth
While you are so far from me?

Even during my loneliness, I still feel your
love, the warmth of your love is here
within me in my heart.

Can you still say you love me even
Though we are so far apart.

Let the heavens and stars guide us together
Till the ends of the world

I'll forever love you

…My Lonely Star…

## Love Me like you Love you

Have you ever been in so deep with
someone you love with all your heart.
But No matter how hard you show them,
your love seems like it's nothing but an
Illusion?

There are no smoking mirrors in front of
You baby.
It's just me with my heart on my
Sleeves wanting you to love me with
All your heart...mind...and even soul.

Can you love me like you say love me, in the
way you tell me every time we are together
While laid up looking at each other?

Let me in your world you see within your eyes
Baby, I feel like an outsider when I should
Feel like your queen and only your queen

The words you say, when you don't really care
Weigh on me in my mind, I wonder while I
Rest do you really love me...

Your actions match your words but
Do the feeling match everything else
You say to me

Am I really the one you deserve for
Or will I be temporary for the time being

# feels of Unwanted Love

Can you see me right in front of you,
While the tears roll down my face?
Will you forever sit there with no expression
upon your face?

Will I forever be just a home girl to you?
Why can't you just let me love you unconditional?

stop fighting your feelings, cause the only
feelings you are stopping are mines
from loving you

My tears won't stop until my last breath
is with you but seem like my last breath
is now.

I'll forever holds you close to my heart even
If it's the one that's taking my last breath
Away.

No one can replace the love
I have for you so stop fighting the love
We have for each other

Let's ride this wave out until we
reach the shore together

Baby… you are my only lover

... Only best friend...
You are my world so let's stay together

...Can we baby...